T0208793

IMAGES

DANITA STEWART

authorHOUSE®

AuthorHouse™
1663 Liberty Drive
Bloomington, IN 47403
www.authorhouse.com
Phone: 1 (800) 839-8640

Published by AuthorHouse   06/12/2020

ISBN: 978-1-7283-6498-8 (sc)
ISBN: 978-1-7283-6497-1 (e)

Print information available on the last page.

Any people depicted in stock imagery provided by Getty Images are models, and such images are being used for illustrative purposes only. Certain stock imagery © Getty Images.

This book is printed on acid-free paper.

Because of the dynamic nature of the Internet, any web addresses or links contained in this book may have changed since publication and may no longer be valid. The views expressed in this work are solely those of the author and do not necessarily reflect the views of the publisher, and the publisher hereby disclaims any responsibility for them.

A Promise

This promise I make to you,
Will be forever true.
I give all my heart,
To only you.
Words cannot even explain,
The way you make me feel.
I know these feelings,
Will always be real.
I love you so much,
We will never part.
You were the one for me,
From the very start.
The bond between us,
You are always there.
The things you do and say,
Show me how much you care.
Together me and you,
Will be as one.
With you by my side,
Anything can be done.
I am telling you this,
From my heart.
I will be with you,
Until death do us part.

You Are The One For Me

You are the one for me,
Forever will be true.
You are the one for me,
I am the one for you.
You are the one for me,
I knew from the start.
You are the one for me,
And always in my heart.
You are the one for me,
This you know.
You are the one for me,
I will never let you go.
You are the one for me,
To talk to and understand.
You are the one for me,
Always will be my man.

He Is In My Corner

No matter how far,
No matter how near.
He is in my corner,
And will always be there.
When I am awake,
Or even asleep.
He is in my corner,
Every day of the week.
He brings me joy,
When there is so much pain.
He releases my sorrows,
When my tears fall like rain.
God sent you,
From heaven above.
To have and to hold,
And specially to love.
He will be there for me,
When I laugh and when I cry,
He is in my corner,
Until the day that I die.

Waiting

I am waiting for the day,
You tell me you love me.
I am waiting for the day,
That forever as one we will be.
I am waiting for the day,
You hold me close to you.
I am waiting for the day,
I can hold you too.
I am waiting for the day,
You ask me to marry.
I am waiting for the day,
For your baby I shall carry.
I am waiting for the day,
I can hear you say I love you.
I am waiting for the day.
We can both say I do.

Unconditional Love

Love has no boundaries,
This we can see.
The fireworks we have,
It will always be.
I want you,
To have and to hold.
To be with me,
Forever as we grow old.
It feels so good when we make love,
I never want that to end.
With you by my side,
I can always win.
I know that,
God sent you from above.
This feeling I have,
Is called an unconditional love.

What Is Love?

Love is a feeling,
That comes from the heart.
Love is when,
You never want to be apart.
Love is caring,
And always being there.
Love is wonderful,
With the right person to share.
Love is being hurt,
And feeling lots of pain.
Love is betrayal,
And being called names.
Love is confusion,
Something everyone knows.
Love can be there,
Or it can go.
Will anyone find,
Love from above.
Does anyone know,
What is love?

Just For You

I want to be the one,
That you come to.
I want to be the one,
Who says I love you.
I want to be the one,
Who says sweet things in your ear.
I want to be the one,
Who will always be there.
I want to be the one,
You will always love.
I want to be the one,
That came from above.
I want to be the one,
That you make love to.
I want to be the one,
Just for you.

Promises

We began as friends,
I wanted so much more.
I wanted to see,
What you had in store.
As we got closer,
We began to see.
That me and you together,
Were meant to be.
The promises we made,
Will stay forever true.
Because the way I feel,
My love is just for you.
I knew it was you,
From the very start.
You will always be,
Forever in my heart.

In Love

To love someone,
Is a great thing.
To see the joys,
It could bring.
To say you love someone,
It must be true.
I cannot deny,
The feelings I have for you.
I never thought,
I could feel so good.
To be with you,
Like I know I should.
We will be,
In love forever.
We will,
Always stay together.

Together Forever

Never being apart,
Always in my heart.
Spending time with me,
And loving me.
Standing by me through it all,
Always there when I call.
Guiding me through tough times,
Helping me rain or shine.
I feel so safe being with you,
I will be loving you forever true.
We will part never,
Until death do us part together forever.

Missing You

The times we spend,
I do adore.
I wish I could,
See you more.
I am so alone,
You know what to do.
Why don't you call,
Are you not thinking of me to?
I do like you a lot,
And I know you like me.
I want us to be,
Together for an eternity.
I want to be,
In your arms kissing you,
I am in depression,
As I am missing you.

Destiny

In our future,
I see a good start.
No matter what happens,
You are always in my heart.
It was fate,
That brought us together.
It is our destiny,
To be together forever.
There are no words,
Which explain the way I feel.
I love you so much,
You know the feelings are real.
Forever,
We will be.
Because it is,
In our destiny.

A True Friend

What is a true friend?
A true friend is someone,
Who shows how much they care.
Who will do things for you,
And always be there.
A true friend can be counted on through thick and thin,
They will make you feel like whatever you do you can win.
The bond between you and that true friend go deep,
It is a type of friendship that lasts longer than a week.
A true friend is hard to find,
But when you do.
Make sure that you,
Will be forever true.

The Perfect Guy

Who would have known,
That you and I would last.
After all the things,
We have shared through the past.
I can still remember,
The first day that we met.
And the first time,
You held me as I wept.
We have made promises,
That will be forever true.
You are the perfect guy for me,
It shows in everything you do.
I will always be the one,
You can count on to be there.
I will show you in all ways,
How much I do care.
I will love you always,
Because you are my perfect guy.

Love Of My Life

I finally found a good man,
That I can love.
God, had to have,
Sent him to me from up above.
The way I feel for him,
Will always remain the same.
The love he has for me,
I hope will never change.
He is someone,
Who I always want around.
He knows how to make me happy,
When I am feeling down.
I feel a bond between us,
That gets deeper and deeper.
I know he is the one,
Who will always be a keeper.
I love him,
More than anything.
When I hear his voice and see his smile,
It makes my heart sing.
I know he is the one for me,
And it seems he feels the same way.
Until the right time,
I will continue to take it day by day.

Untitled

You told me,
You would always be there.
You use to show,
How much you cared.
Now all you do,
Is tell me lies.
But do not worry,
There will be no cries.
So many times,
You abandoned me.
This was coming,
Yes, I did see.
When you decided to change,
That was the end.
Of what you were,
A wonderful friend.

Lifetime

A lifetime together,
We will have.
Full of tears,
Full of laughs.
So many memories,
We will share.
Keeping many promises,
Which are very dear.
Our love grows,
Stronger and stronger.
As the days become,
Longer and longer.
Cherishing precious moments,
That will always remain.
Holding each other close,
As we whisper each other's name.

Our Friendship

When we first met,
I would have never thought it would be.
You told me things and gave me advice,
You made me open my eyes and see.
That a true friend,
Will always be there.
Through thick and thin,
Showing how much she cares.
You have been with me,
Through all the god times and the bad.
When I was unhappy,
You knew how to make me glad.
Even though we stopped talking for a while,
We both put that in the past.
And now we talk like we use to,
We both know this will last.
Before I end this poem,
There is one thing I must say.
I am glad we met,
And friend I love you every day.

A Special Friend

In you I have found,
A friend I always want to be around.
When I was mad, you were still there,
You make me happy while wiping away my tears.
I am lucky to have found a friend like you,
You will never change, you will always be true.
I am glad our friendship did begin,
We have a special friendship that I always wanted to have.
You are caring, sensitive, funny and can always make me laugh.
The way I feel words cannot explain,
I can tell by your eyes that you feel the same.
In you I see a special friend,
With you by my side I can always win.

Husband

Like a knight in shiny armor,
You came into my life.
From the look in your eyes,
I knew one day I would be your wife.
I have been so happy,
Since our very first date.
The bond that we shared,
You are the perfect mate.
With mind, body and soul,
I will love you.
Through good times and bad,
I will be forever true.

The Surprise

What is a surprise?
It could make you happy,
It could make you sad.
It could make you feel good,
It could make you mad.
The surprise..........
A diamond ring,
Which will be forever.
A promise of love,
We will share together.
The surprise.........
A break-up,
My heart is broken again.
Why couldn't I see,
That this was the end.
The surprise...........
A pregnancy,
The joy it brings.
A boy or a girl,
We will sing.

Unwanted

I think back to the time,
When the condom broke.
The pregnancy read positive,
I almost choked.
The father of the baby,
Left me in a bind.
I did not know what to do,
I was running out of time.
I never thought,
It could happen to me.
But now I know,
It can be.
Should I kill it,
Because of my mistake.
Or should I keep it,
With all the time it will take.
I went through,
The abortion I wanted.
I could not give the love,
Because the baby was unwanted.

Stuck

Stuck in the house,
Because of the snow.
Nothing to do,
And nowhere to go.
All I can do,
Is talk on the phone.
Or be depressed,
Because I am so alone.
Should I begin,
To bake a cake.
Or is a good nap,
Something I should take.
This boring day,
Seems like it wants to stay.
Will this snow,
Please go away.

Untitled 2

We have been talking,
For quite a while.
We even know what makes,
Each other smile.
I know we are both scared,
To take that step.
But shouldn't we be happy,
After all that we wept.
Isn't it our turn,
To really enjoy life.
And see if some day,
I will become your wife.
We have stood by each other,
When no one else dared.
We have kissed and talked,
And showed how much we cared.
The love we have,
Can stand up in any kind of weather.
Even though there are some,
Who don't want us together.
Let's take that step,
And become one.
As long as we have each other,
I know anything can be done.

What If?

What if....
> Everything was perfect,
> We were husband and wife.
> We had two children,
> And a very loving life.

What if....
> You were betrayed,
> And accused of lying.
> Would it make you feel?
> Like you were dying.

What if....
> Your ex changed,
> And she made you see.
> That you and her together,
> Should always be.

What if....
> I told you,
> How much I love you.
> Would it make a difference?
> Or would you abandon me too.

What if....
> I told you,
> I did not care how others feel.
> Because the love I have for you,
> Will always be real.

What if....
> You looked at me,
> And said.
> I wish that you,
> Were dead.

What if....
> I tell you,
> Together I want to be
> Then asked you,
> Will you marry me?

What if????

A Dying Love

I had loved you,
Through the good and the bad.
I could even tell,
When you were happy or mad.
I had done nothing,
But show you how much I cared.
Why you could not see,
After all that we have shared.
You had my love,
From the start.
But all you wanted to do,
Was break my heart.
I tried to show you,
In so many ways.
How much I loved you,
And wished you would stay.
But then something happened,
You had had changed.
And I knew then,
Things would never be the same.
We could never go back,
To how it used to be.
So, I gave up,
That is how you lost me.

The Betrayal

Who would have thought,
Something evil you would do.
You acted like a friend,
Who could see through?
All the deception,
And all the lies.
There will be,
No more lonely cries.
Why try to hold on,
To something not there.
It is over,
You were never there.
Shit happens,
Is all that you can say.
A forgotten betrayal,
Day after day.

The Past

I know you have been hurt,
Many times in the past.
I am here to let you know,
It will not last.
I want to be the one,
Who shows you how love can be.
I want to so things for you,
So, the love I have for you is all you see.
On purpose or unintentionally,
I will never hurt you.
I want to make you happy,
In anything that we do.
When you look at me,
I want you to see love in my eyes.
When you think of me,
I want you to know I will be there until the day I die.

The Mistake

You made me feel things,
I should not have felt.
My mind said no,
My heart wanted to melt.
I know I should have never,
Came back in your life.
I had to realize,
I am someone's wife.
I love my man,
That you could not see.
All that you wanted,
Was to be all over me.
If I would have let that happen,
It would have changed my fate.
My world would have been doomed,
By one little mistake.

An Untrue Friend

So many times you were there,
Through all my tears.
Through all the pain and sorrow,
And all the unfriendly stares.
I thought you would be the one,
Who always stood by me.
Betrayal, lies and bad advice,
A true friend you could never be.
We have told so many secrets,
Which were close to my heart.
I know now it was a scheme,
You were out to get me from the start.
Through the good and the bad,
Who thought it would end?
I am glad that I now know,
That you have been an untrue friend.

Unhappy

I can see the sadness in your eyes,
I can hear your lonely cries.
Why must you feel so blue,
What has the world done to you?
Your pain is tearing you apart,
Can you find joy deep in your heart?
I know there is reason for your pain,
Why keep it inside, there is nothing to gain.
I love you and want you to smile,
Can you be happy at least for a while?
If you saw what I could see,
You would not be so unhappy.

Suicide

I remember the time,
When I wanted to commit suicide.
Would anyone care,
If I had died.
I was going through a lot,
No one was there for me.
Through all the rumors and name calling,
I stood strong.
Even if they did not see,
What they were doing wrong.
Do you know how it felt?
To get backstabbed by your closet friends.
Through all this,
I just wanted my life to end.
They talked about me right in my face,
I tried to act like I did not care.
But the pain of it all,
Will always be there.
The hatred I felt,
No one has ever seen,
I did nothing wrong,
Is that why they acted so mean.

The Deadly Touch

You said that,
You would always love me.
You told me,
We were meant to be.
You swindled your way in,
You played with my heart.
I should have,
Seen it from the very start.
We kissed and touched,
And fooled around.
Now I find out,
I will be deep underground.
You told me,
I could trust you,
You had HIV,
And now I have it too.
You gave me something,
That will not ever go away.
You plead and plead,
But there is nothing left to say.

Hurt

You did not see the pain,
When you look in my eyes.
They are crying out,
But you did not hear my cries.
I am starting to wonder,
How long it will last.
Cause I have been hurt,
Many times in the past.
Deep inside all I want,
Is to find the right one.
But the guys I have known make me have doubts,
Will this guy ever come?
Why do people call me names?
I just want to be left be.
No one understands how I feel,
But I do wish that they could see.
Sometimes when I am sitting alone,
I feel the need to cry.
People sometimes make me feel,
That they wish I would die.
I try to be strong,
But all I see is pain.
I wish the time would go back,
But I know it would never be the same.

Molested

You feel so dirty,
How could this have happened.
You did not say anything,
Cause you feel so frightened.
You blame yourself,
Cause you let it happen over and over again.
You cannot keep quiet,
You tell at least one friend.
Each time it happens,
It feels worse and worse.
You feel the pain,
You see the blood when it burst.
Oh! Lord you say,
Why me?
Did I deserve this,
Why couldn't he leave me be?
Do not ever joke, -
About being molested.
If it happens to you,
Go as soon as possible to get tested.

Don't Judge Me

I am human I do have feelings too,
Do not judge me just because I am not like you.
I am true to myself, I do not try to impress,
Do not talk behind my back about the way that I dress.
I could care less what you think of me,
You do not have to look my way just let me be.
I have not done anything to you,
Be nice for a change and we can start a new.
My true feelings I do hide,
I could be the best friend you ever had,
But if you do not want that I will not be sad.
I do not really know what about me upsets you,
Why don't you tell me, what it is that I do?
Read this poem, you can see,
That all I am saying is do not judge me.

Brokenhearted

As I sit alone,
I feel the need to cry.
I try to say I am alright,
But it is all one big lie.
I am so sad,
Can't you see I love you.
I want you back,
Cause boy I really do need you.
I thought we had,
A love that would never end.
I only had eyes for you,
Because you were my boyfriend.
Why you left me,
I will never understand.
All I ever wanted,
Was you as my man.
At one point,
You were all mine.
Then you were gone,
I had run out of time.
The way you made me feel,
I really do miss.
Before we say good-bye,
Can I get one last kiss?
When we broke up,
I was so brokenhearted.
I had never dreamed,
That one day we would have parted.
Baby will you please,
Open your eyes and see.
That me and you together,
Will always be meant to be.

The Roommate

You open the door,
To let her in.
Who would have known,
You could not be friends.
So many days,
You wanted to scream and yell.
Wishing your roommate,
Would go to hell.
The way she is,
You cannot stand.
Why does she?
Always brag about her man.
You try to act,
As if she is your friend.
All the while hoping,
Will this please end.

Lonely

To be alone,
In a world so cold.
Is like,
Having your life on hold.
You may have friends,
But you do not feel that way.
Where are the people,
That you need to stay.
You do not like,
This feeling inside.
It is all like,
One bumpy ride.
You think to yourself,
Is it me only?
Am I the one,
Who always feel so lonely?

A Secret Affair

This secret affair,
We began as friends.
Now what we have,
We do not want to end.
There is someone else,
In both our lives.
But we cannot stop,
Cause it feels so right.
I know I should not,
But I do like you.
There are things,
I would like to do.
If only we were single,
We could be together.
To have and to hold,
Forever and ever.

Anger

There is an anger,
Building up inside of me.
I hide my feelings,
So that no one will see.
The pain I felt,
And will feel again.
Is the kind of pain,
That will never end.
Why doesn't anyone,
Talk to me.
Do I?
Intimidate thee.
I sit and ponder,
About the situation.
With so much anger inside,
I will never win.

Why?

As I sit,
Alone to cry.
I ask myself,
I wonder why.
Even when you,
Have close friends.
You can feel,
Life coming to an end.
As your heart breaks,
You feel the pain.
People need to realize,
This is not a game.
Why me?
Is all I can say.
Can I be accepted?
In any kind of way.

Lies

To tell the truth,
Would be hard for you.
Does it hurt?
Knowing what you say is not true.
No one will like you,
If you keep lying.
Will you stop,
Are you even trying?
Each time you lie,
You lose a friend.
Is this how?
You want to win.
Through all the pain,
And your cries.
You continue,
To tell lies.

Used

Once again I feel so used,
This just gives me the blues.
I gave you all that I could give,
I would give you my heart if it would help you live.
I really do care about you,
But you do not see how much I really do.
I am trying to show you things will be different,
Don't you feel we were meant.
I know you have been hurt in the past,
But you need to remember it will not last.
You gave me your friendship I did accept,
You used me over and over as I wept.
I have seen so many clues,
And now I am telling you I refuse to be used.
Never again will I let someone use me,
It is not a good thing, that you should see.

A Secret Pain

You have made many promises,
You never kept.
You were not there for me,
When I wept.
You said we would fall in love,
I thought it would be.
Then you stopped calling,
That really hurt me.
You try to come back,
With one little kiss.
You cannot make up,
For all that you missed.
Yes, I did care,
You say you did not know.
It was obvious,
This I did show.
By doing this,
There was nothing to gain.
If only you saw,
My secret pain.

The Journey

Do you say what you mean?
And mean what you say.
Are you loyal and honest?
Do you show integrity every day?
Are you in this for the long haul?
Or are you playing with my heart.
It was a strong connection,
Right from the start.
Our friendship deepens,
As we take our time.
Is there a future?
Will you be mine?
Only time can tell,
What God has in store.
Our journey will begin,
We both deserve more.
Do we take this step together?
Yes, because you are my mate.
The future we can have,
Will be great.
It is time to take a chance,
And become who you were meant to be.
None of the others wanted to wait,
I Stayed because of the greatness I see.
You are destined for more,
Your dreams can come true.
I am behind you all the way,
Cause I believe in you.

Invisible

Damaged, hurt, and confused,
Feelings inside of me.
Tears I cry,
Why can't you see?
The frustrations of life,
Will anyone ever notice me?
The pain I feel each day,
This is not how life should be.
The feeling of loneliness that never leaves,
Am I thought of at all?
I try to be the best I can be,
Most days I will not get one single call.
Am I to be alone?
No one to love, no one to care.
Can I be loved?
Or is this the future I must bare?
You ask if I am okay,
I say that I am fine.
Don't you see I am crying out?
Are you really that blind?
Can't you see?
The pain in my eyes.
Or is it?
You want to believe the lies.
I am human, I have feelings,
But to all I am invisible.

Friend

A friend should be:
Someone you can count on,
Someone you can trust.
Someone you can confide in,
Loyalty is a must.
Someone you can share with,
Someone you can lean on.
When time gets rough,
Someone that is always by your side.
That knows you inside and out.
Someone that cares,
Someone you never have to doubt.
A friend is someone:
Who knows when you need to talk,
They always call at the perfect time.
As if they know you were depressed,
You can count on them,
They have passed the test.
A true friend will always be there,
Everyone needs that in their life.
Without the friendship,
Nothing will ever go right.
A friend should never betray you,
Love that type of friend.
And you will have,
Happiness until the end.
A friend is a blessing,
You should not take for granted.
A friend is real, honest and funny,
One of God's great gifts.

Untitled

It is time for this pain to end,
I cannot take it no more.
I want to die,
What does God have in store?
Am I loved? Or am I hated?
I really need to know.
Are my flaws unattractive?
Or am I accepted as so?
Will you ever show me?
What I need to see?
How should I act?
Who am I supposed to be?

The Proposal

Two people meet,
A connection is made.
Their hearts are entwined,
With a love that will not fade.
They enjoy each other,
And always have fun.
It did not dawn on them,
They had found the "one."
It took a while for them to see,
Their damaged hearts had to heal.
But once it did,
They realized what they have is real.
The proposal came,
As a real shock.
She could not believe,
The size of the rock,
Yes, I will be your wife,
To love forever and ever.
They became one,
Together they will be, unbroken never.

Perserverance

Do not be scared,
Step out on faith.
It is your time,
No time to wait.
Be the star,
You are supposed to be.
Leave the past behind,
I am with you, don't you see.
If you keep waiting,
Your dreams will not come true.
Stop talking and make things happen,
Remember everyone will not be rooting for you.
Stand up and press on,
You already planted the seed.
Be the boss,
You know what you need.
Do not keep waiting,
The right time may never come.
Go get what is yours,
It is time to get things done.
Do not fear,
God has got you.

Did You?

Did you?
Think we were that cool.
That I was a complete fool.
Did you?
Know that I had no respect for you,
That I was just using you.
Did you?
Think your lies were so believable.
That you could play with my heart,
I knew the type of man you were from the start.
Are you?
So broken that you did not see,
That really the relationship was about me.
Are you?
That much of a loser you stayed in the past,
Everything you did just made you look like an ass.
Do you?
Know when to take a stand,
That you need to learn how to be a real man.
Do you?
Know how it may feel,
When people do not keep it real.
Do you?
Know that I am invisible.

Doomed

America is so screwed up,
But what can we do?
People always thinking,
They are better than you.
We say black lives matter,
Is that really true?
The racism and the hatred,
Are a little part of you.
When will this stop,
We need to come together.
Start thinking of your fellow man,
Or are we doomed forever.
The power of the tongue can be death,
Lies being told.
Same thing on the news,
Isn't this getting old?
Parents do you care?
That kids are growing up to fast.
You let them watch and listen,
To all this trash.
Wake up America,
We need to find a new way,
Can we stick together?
Let's take this day by day.

Printed in the United States
By Bookmasters